1996 E   Suggested Solutions

Constitutional Law

LLB

University of London External Examinations

Solutions by Jonathan Miller
LLB, Dip Int Rel, LLM

HLT Publications

HLT PUBLICATIONS
200 Greyhound Road, London W14 9RY

Examination Questions © The University of London 1996
Solutions © The HLT Group Ltd 1996
Reprinted 1999

All HLT publications enjoy copyright protection and the copyright belongs to The HLT Group Ltd.

All rights reserved. No part of this publication may be reproduced or transmitted in any form or by any means, electronic, mechanical, photocopying, recording or otherwise, or stored in any retrieval system of any nature without either the written permission of the copyright holder, application for which should be made to The HLT Group Ltd, or a licence permitting restricted copying in the United Kingdom issued by the Copyright Licensing Agency.

Any person who infringes the above in relation to this publication may be liable to criminal prosecution and civil claims for damages.

ISBN 0 7510 0751 X

British Library Cataloguing-in-Publication.

A CIP Catalogue record for this book is available from the British Library.

Printed and bound in Great Britain.

CONTENTS

Acknowledgement   v

Introduction   vii

Examination Paper   3

Suggested Solutions

    Question 1   9

    Question 2   15

    Question 3   21

    Question 4   29

    Question 5   35

    Question 6   41

    Question 7   49

    Question 8   55

ACKNOWLEDGEMENT

The questions used are taken from the University of London LLB (External) Degree examination paper and our thanks are extended to the University of London for the kind permission which has been given to us to use and publish the questions.

Caveat

The answers given are not approved or sanctioned by the University of London and are entirely our responsibility.

They are not intended as 'Model Answers', but rather as Suggested Solutions.

The answers have two fundamental purposes, namely:

a) To provide a detailed example of a suggested solution to examination questions, and

b) To assist students with their research into the subject and to further their understanding and appreciation of the subject.

Note

Please note that the solutions in this book were written in the year of the examination. They were appropriate solutions at the time of preparation, but students must note that certain caselaw and statutes may subsequently have changed.

INTRODUCTION

Why choose HLT publications?

Holborn College has earned an international reputation for the outstanding quality of its teaching, Textbooks, Casebooks and Suggested Solutions to past examination papers.

Our expertise is reflected in the outstanding results achieved by our students in the examinations conducted by the University of London LLB Honours Degree Programme for External Students, the Council of Legal Education, and by students in over 70 universities who use our publications.

Suggested Solutions

The Suggested Solutions series provides examples of full answers to the problems posed by examiners. The solutions are much more than answers achievable by a candidate under examination conditions. The opportunity has been taken, where appropriate, to develop themes, suggest alternatives and set out additional material providing further comprehensive topical coverage.

To aid comprehension and revision, the solutions are fuller than would be possible under examination conditions. It is important to keep in mind that at this level there almost certainly is more than just one approach in answering any given question.

We feel that in writing full opinion answers we can assist you with your research and further your understanding and appreciation of the law.

Notes on examination technique

Although the SUBSTANCE and SLANT of the answer changes according to the subject-matter of the question, the examining body and syllabus concerned, the TECHNIQUE of answering examination questions does not change.

You will not pass an examination if you do not know the substance of a course. You may pass if you do not know how to go about answering a question although this is doubtful. To do well and to guarantee success, however, it is necessary to learn the technique of answering problems properly. The following is a guide to acquiring that technique.

Time

All examinations permit only a limited time for papers to be completed. All papers require you to answer a certain number of questions in that time, and the questions, with some exceptions carry equal marks.

It follows from this that you should never spend a disproportionate amount of time on any question. When you have used up the amount of time allowed for any one question STOP and go on to the next question after an abrupt conclusion, if necessary. If you feel that you are running out of time, then complete your answer in note form. A useful way of ensuring that you do not over-run is to write down on a piece of scrap paper the time at which you should be starting each part of the paper. This can be done in the few minutes before the examination begins and it will help you to calm any nerves you may have.

Reading the question

It will not be often that you will be able to answer every question on an examination paper. Inevitably, there will be some areas in which you feel better prepared than others. You will prefer to answer the questions which deal with those areas, but you will never know how good the questions are unless you read the whole examination paper.

You should spend at least 10 MINUTES at the beginning of the examination reading the questions. Preferably, you should read them more than once. As you go through each question, make a brief note on the examination paper of any relevant cases and/or statutes that occur to you even if you think you may not answer that question: you may well be grateful for this note towards the end of the examination when you are tired and your memory begins to fail.

Re-reading the answers

Ideally, you should allow time to re-read your answers. This is rarely a pleasant process, but will ensure that you do not make any silly mistakes such as leaving out a 'not' when the negative is vital.

The structure of the answer

Almost all examination problems raise more than one legal issue that you are required to deal with. Your answer should:

Identify the issues raised by the question
This is of crucial importance and gives shape to the whole answer. It indicates to the examiner that you appreciate what he is asking you about.

This is at least as important as actually answering the questions of law raised by that issue.

The issues should be identified in the first paragraph of the answer.

Deal with those issues one by one as they arise in the course of the problem
This, of course, is the substance of the answer and where study and revision pays off.

If the answer to an issue turns on a provision of a statute, CITE that provision briefly, but do not quote it from any statute you may be permitted to bring into the examination hall
Having cited the provision, show how it is relevant to the question.

If there is no statute, or the meaning of the statute has been interpreted by the courts, CITE the relevant cases
'Citing cases' does not mean writing down the name of every case that happens to deal with the general topic with which you are concerned and then detailing all the facts you can think of.

You should cite only the most relevant cases – there may perhaps only be one. No more facts should be stated than are absolutely essential to establish the relevance of the case. If there is a relevant case, but you cannot remember its name, it is sufficient to refer to it as 'one decided case'.

Whenever a statute or case is cited, the title of statute or the name of the case should be underlined
This makes the examiner's job much easier because he can see at a glance whether the relevant material has been dealt with, and it will make him more disposed in your favour.

Having dealt with the relevant issues, summarise your conclusions in such a way that you answer the question
A question will often say at the end simply 'Advise A', or B, or C, etc. The advice will usually turn on the individual answers to a number of issues. The point made here is that the final paragraph should pull those individual answers together and actually give the advice required. For example, it may begin something like: 'The effect of the answer to the issues raised by this question is that one's advice to A is that ...'

Related to the previous paragraph, make sure at the end that you have answered the question

For example, if the question says 'Advise A', make sure that is what your answer does. If you are required to advise more than one party, make sure that you have dealt with all the parties that you are required to and no more.

Some general points

You should always try to get the examiner on your side. One method has already been mentioned – the underlining of case names, etc. There are also other ways as well.

Always write as neatly as you can. This is more easily done with ink than with a ball-point.

Avoid the use of violently coloured ink eg turquoise; this makes a paper difficult to read.

Space out your answers sensibly: leave a line between paragraphs. You can always get more paper. At the same time, try not to use so much paper that your answer book looks too formidable to mark. This is a question of personal judgment.

NEVER put in irrelevant material simply to show that you are clever. Irrelevance is not a virtue and time spent on it is time lost for other, relevant, answers.

EXAMINATION PAPER

UNIVERSITY OF LONDON
LLB EXAMINATIONS 1996
for External Students
INTERMEDIATE EXAMINATION (Scheme A)
FIRST AND SECOND YEAR EXAMINATIONS (Scheme B)
GRADUATE ENTRY LEVEL I (Route A)
GRADUATE ENTRY FIRST YEAR (Route B)

CONSTITUTIONAL LAW

Tuesday, 4 June: 10.00 am to 1.00 pm

Answer *FOUR* of the following EIGHT questions

1   In what respects does the British Constitution conform to, or contradict, the doctrine of separation of powers?

2   Discuss the nature and effect of the constitutional conventions which regulate the public conduct of the Sovereign as Head of State in the United Kingdom.

3   Consider the view that 'our method of election to the House of Commons is in the highest degree unjust, unsatisfactory and dangerous'.

4   Discuss, by reference to decided cases, the legal status of European Community law within the United Kingdom and its priority in relation to provisions in domestic Acts of Parliament.

5   Article 11 of the European Convention on Human Rights provides that 'Everyone has the right to peaceful assembly'. How is this human right guaranteed in English Law?

6   Compare and contrast the effectiveness of judicial and parliamentary controls over the exercise of prerogative executive powers by government ministers.

7   Discuss the range of legal powers by which central government controls the actions of local authorities.

8   Section 2 of the (fictitious) National Health Act 1996, provides that Area Health Authorities 'are under a duty to maintain adequate hospital beds and services to ensure the protection and maintenance of the health of residents in the area'.

In January 1996, the (fictitious) Western Area Health Authority, in an effort to cut costs, decided to close two hospital wards usually reserved for elderly patients requiring long-term care, and a ward containing ten beds reserved for patients in need of either pre- or post-operative intensive care.

In April 1996, Mrs Jones, who is elderly and has no living relatives to care for her, was admitted to the Wellbeing Hospital, a national health service hospital in the Western area. In June, however, Mr Smith, a hospital administrator, notified Mrs Jones that she would have to leave hospital within a week, even though she could not care for herself.

In February 1996, Toby, who is six years old, was found to be suffering from a rare bone marrow disease. The Wellbeing Hospital has refused to admit Toby for urgent surgery because of the shortage of beds. His mother, Mrs Jones, has been told that he will have to wait 'for up to three months' for the necessary surgery. She has consulted another doctor, who is a family friend, who has advised her that the delay in treatment could seriously affect Toby's chances of a full recovery from the disease.

Advise Mrs Brown and Mrs Jones as to whether they are entitled to seek a remedy by way of an action for judicial review, and as to the likely outcome of any judicial review proceedings.

SUGGESTED SOLUTIONS

QUESTION 1

In what respects does the British Constitution conform to, or contradict, the doctrine of separation of powers?

SUGGESTED SOLUTION TO QUESTION 1

General Comment

The question involves an understanding of the basic structure and workings of the British Constitution.

The candidate should be familiar with what is meant by the doctrine of separation of powers and how this idea is put into practice in the context of the unwritten constitution of the United Kingdom. This will also involve an appreciation of the workings of conventions and the role of important 'actors' in the constitution.

Skeleton Solution

Definition of the doctrine.

Its strict application in other constitutional jurisdictions, eg the US.

Relevance to the UK; the Westminster model – the comments of Bagehot – the role and functions of the Attorney-General, Lord Chancellor, the Law Lords.

In contradistinction, the independence of the judiciary, Act of Settlement, House of Commons Disqualification Act 1975 and the judiciary.

The status of the Crown.

Conclusion.

Suggested Solution

The doctrine of separation of powers divides the workings of a constitution into three distinct branches. These are the legislature, the executive and the judiciary. The legislature passes the laws, the executive puts them into practice and the judiciary interprets them. The 'highpoint' of this doctrine is to be found in the works of the eighteenth century philosopher Montesquieu. In this book *The Spirit of the Laws*, published in 1748, the author advances the view that the best foundation for individual liberty and good governance is to separate the three branches of government. The three branches of government will have distinct functions and none will be powerful enough to dominate the others.

Montesquieu wrongly believed that this formula applied to the England of his time, but the theory served to influence the founding fathers of the American constitution, which does apply the doctrine in practice. A member of the United States Congress is forbidden, for example, to be a member of the United States government: art 1, s6.

How, then, is this doctrine relevant to the UK? First, the United Kingdom constitution is characterised by the blending of the executive and the legislature. It is unusual, as a result of constitutional conventional practice, for a member of the executive *not* to be a member of the legislature. If the government of the day wishes to bring in an outsider – a non-professional politician – into government then that individual must be found a seat in the legislature, either in the House of Commons through election or in the House of Lords through ennoblement. Walter Bagehot in his classical work *The English Constitution* (1867) describes the constitution as displaying 'the close union, the nearly complete fusion of the executive and legislative powers'.

He then went on to argue that the fusion takes place in the Cabinet, a body which he graphically described as:

> 'a combining committee – a hyphen which joins a buckle which fastens the legislative part of the state to the executive part of the state. In its origin it belongs to the one, in its functions it belongs to another'.

The Cabinet and government only come into existence because the majority of the legislature wish it so, but, as Bagehot points out, the Cabinet (and now the Prime Minister) may request a dissolution of Parliament and 'annihilate the legislature'. In contrast, the United States' President cannot dissolve the Congress, nor is his existence dependent upon a majority in the legislature. The amalgamation of the executive and the legislature and the answerability of the executive to the legislature, demonstrated in Question Time, is one of the fundamental characteristics of the Westminister model of government.

The role and functions of particular offices in government display this amalgamation of the branches of government. The Attorney-General has a function as a quasi-judicial officer of the Crown. In this role he decides in a limited number of offences and cases whether or not to initiate a prosecution. In this he is answerable to Parliament – usually the House of Commons – and may in theory be removed by them in a vote of no confidence. The Attorney-General is a member of the government, although not a member of the Cabinet, a convention which resulted from the alleged pressure which was placed upon the then Attorney-General, Sir Patrick Hastings, who withdrew a prosecuting against J R Campbell, acting editor of a Communist paper, for 'incitement to mutiny'. The Attorney-General does take into account the views of the Cabinet when performing his functions, but he is not bound by the views of the Cabinet or Prime Minister. When Lord Denning, in an inventive phase, tried to make the Attorney-General answerable to the courts, this was firmly repudiated by the House of Lords in *Gouriet* v *Union of Post Office Workers* (1). Similarly, the Divisional Court in *R* v *Solicitor-General, ex parte Taylor* (2) reiterated that the Attorney-General, or the Solicitor-General acting on his behalf, is not amenable to judicial review of his official decisions.

It is with the officer of Lord Chancellor that the absence of separation of powers is most marked. The Lord Chancellor is a member not only of the government but also of the Cabinet. He is chosen by the Prime Minister, and previous Lord Chancellors, such as Lord Hailsham, have had an active political career before ascending to the office. Indeed, Lord Hailsham once ran for the leadership of the Conservative Party. The Lord Chancellor has important administrative functions to perform in connection with the judiciary and is responsible for law reform, some of which may be politically controversial, as with Lord Mackay's proposed reform of the divorce laws. The Lord Chancellor is also a judge and may preside over the judicial committee of the House of Lords. This office also entitles the holder to sit in the legislature (in the House of Lords), and the Lord Chancellor acts as Speaker of the upper chamber, performing a Janus-type role of acting as an umpire – although less active than the House of Commons Speaker – and participant. The Lord Chancellor is also instrumental in the appointment of members of the judiciary in practice and theory. Justices of the Peace (JPs) are appointed by the Lord Chancellor on the advice of local advisory committees. Without the benefit of an advisory committee he appoints, for instance, High Court judges, Circuit Judges and Recorders. He also has the power to remove members of the judiciary below the status of superior court judges.

While an adherence to the doctrine of separation of powers would imply the disconnection of the judiciary and the legislature this is *not* found with regard to the role of the Lords of Appeal in Ordinary. The Law Lords can and do play a part in the proceedings of the upper chamber, and while it used to be correct to say that they avoided politically controversial issues, this is not now strictly the case. The response of Lord Taylor, the then Lord Chief Justice, in 1996 to the Home Secretary's proposed reform of sentencing casts doubt over the previously accepted view.

Considering the above discussion then how may Lord Diplock accurately state that 'the British Constitution is firmly based upon the separation of powers' (3)? Presumably what is meant by this statement is the adherence to the concept of the independence of the judiciary. The Act of Settlement 1700 provided that the superior court judges should hold office upon 'good behaviour' rather than the 'King's pleasure' as had been the case. The independence of the judiciary and the inability of the executive to remove them is one of the hallmarks of the separation of powers. Since 1700 superior court judges can only be removed by the Crown on an address presented to it by both Houses of Parliament. It has to be said, however, that Circuit Judges and Recorders may be removed from office by the Lord Chancellor for 'inability or misbehaviour'.

Also, in accordance with the separation of the judiciary from the legislature and the executive is the statutory prohibition of full time members of the judiciary from the House of Commons: House of Commons Disqualification Act 1967.

All of the above, of course, is based upon the conventional (in the technical sense) role of the monarchy. While the Queen is forbidden to enter the House of Commons this is of little or no practical significance as her Ministers dominate the chamber. One may nevertheless conclude that although under the Westminister model the theory of separation of powers is more honoured in the breach than the observance; nevertheless the adherence to the practice of the independence of the judiciary has meant that the courts may maintain an independent and separate existence from the law-makers.

References

(1) [1977] 3 All ER 70
(2) (1995) The Times 14 August
(3) *Duport Steel v Sirs* [1980] 1 WLR 142

QUESTION 2

Discuss the nature and effect of the constitutional conventions which regulate the public conduct of the Sovereign as Head of State in the United Kingdom.

SUGGESTED SOLUTION TO QUESTION 2

General Comment

This is a rather narrow question. It involves the role of the sovereign and is not an opportunity to repeat the material dealing with the executive use of the prerogative which needs to be discussed in the answer to Question 6.

An understanding of the term 'convention(s)' is required. The candidate should also be able to discuss such issues as the appointment and dismissal of the Prime Minister and the related issue of the dissolution of Parliament. Historical examples are necessary when dealing with the influence of conventions upon the role of the monarchy. Also some knowledge of the 1975 Australian constitutional crisis would be useful.

Skeleton Solution

Definition of conventions.

Royal assent to Bills.

Apportionment of ministers and the Prime Minister.

Dissolution of Parliament.

Conclusion.

Suggested Solution

Constitutional conventions have been described by Dicey (1) as:

> 'understandings, habits or practices ... which are not in reality laws at all since they are not enforced by the courts'.

They do, however, make sense of the constitution, and in the words of Sir Ivor Jennings (2):

> '... they provide the flesh which clothes the dry bones of the law; they make the legal constitution work ...'

This is particularly true of the role of the monarch. The powers of the Head of State are limited by convention, and in the majority of cases the functions of the monarch have passed into the hands of other actors of the constitution or else the monarch has no discretion on how to act. This is correct, for example, at the basic level of how statutes come into existence. When a Bill has passed both House of Parliament (the Parliament Acts notwithstanding) the monarch is obliged to give it Royal Assent, or so the convention would indicate. The position is, however, slightly clouded when one looks at past events in constitutional history. The classic textbook example is that of Queen Anne in 1708 refusing to give her assent to the Scottish Militia Bill, thus seeming to indicate that the monarch is not obliged by convention to assent to each and every Bill. The facts are, however, somewhat more opaque in that not only did her ministers not object but in fact they rather approved of this course of action. In more recent times the issue was resurrected over the question of Home Rule for Ireland in the period of 1912–14. In April 1912 the Liberal government introduced a Home Rule Bill in the House of Commons, and to avoid the nineteenth century precedent of the Bill being rejected by the House of Lords stated that they would, if necessary, utilise the Parliament Act 1911 to by-pass the House of Lords' veto. The proposed legislation aroused strong opposition amongst the Ulster Protestant community and their supporters, the Conservative Unionists. The King (George V) had the theoretical power to thwart the progress of the Bill by insisting that an election be held before the legislation was passed or by refusing to assent to the Bill. A memorandum was in fact prepared by the King to Prime Minister Asquith but it was never sent because the outbreak of the 1914–18 war. The memorandum indicated that there might be occasions on which the King would be justified in refusing to assent to legislation. When this would occur is not completely clear, but the memorandum indicated that the Crown would only adopt this course of action if it would have the effect of diffusing a crisis. It is doubtful whether in today's political climate the monarch would contemplate such an action, even if proposed legislation would have the effect of abolishing the UK's position as a sovereign state (for instance, proposed legislation to join a federal European Union).

The sovereign (Queen Elizabeth II) has the theoretical power to appoint whoever she wishes as a minister, and she could in theory appoint somebody outside Parliament. In fact her power is regulated by convention, and ministerial appointments are made on the advice of the Prime Minister in relation to individuals who either sit in Parliament (meaning both Houses) or whom it is proposed will sit in Parliament by means of either a successful by-election or an elevation to the peerage. Such a constitutional arrangement does not generate controversy; in greater dispute is the sovereign's power to appoint a Prime Minister.

The Prime Minister (PM) is appointed from the contestants who are able to command an overall majority in the House of Commons. This does not normally present a problem, since because of the workings of the electoral system (3) one party usually commands an overall majority in the House of Commons and it is usually the leader of that party who then becomes PM.

Problems may arise if, for instance, an incumbent PM resigns. In the two leading political parties, Conservative and Labour, a method of electing the next leader is provided for. This was not always the case, and up to 1964 the Conservative Party leader used to 'emerge', which could theoretically leave the monarch with an area of discretion. In 1923 when the Conservative PM Bonar Law resigned, the Conservative Lord Curzon was put forward as his successor, but George V thought it appropriate to appoint the Conservative commoner Baldwin as the Labour Party was unrepresented in the Lords and the King was of the opinion that it would be inappropriate to appoint a peer as PM.

Such an event in unlikely to occur again, but in more recent history the question as to who should be PM was raised again. In February 1974 the election result proved inconclusive as no one party had an overall majority. The incumbent PM, Edward Heath (as he then was), only resigned after spending three days trying to construct a coalition government. The Queen waited until the situation sorted itself out and then called for the main opposition leader, Harold Wilson, to form a government. The possibility of such events repeating themselves would, of course be more likely if electroal reform is introduced and overall majority governments cease to be the norm (4). The role of the monarch in this area would be highlighted and the Queen would be able to exercise a discretionary function.

Of more constitutional significance is th role of the monarch in the dissolution or non-dissolution of Parliament. Whether or not Parliament is dissolved is not in fact governed by convention (contrary to popular belief). The *request* as to the dissolution of Parliament is made, since November 1918, by the PM. The Queen could in theory refuse to grant a dissolution, although this is not likely, particularly as the PM would probably then resign. The converse is also true, and the monarch could insist upon a dissolution of Parliament if the government of the day was planning controversial and unprecedented legislation. The example of George V in the decade before the 1914–18 war is a precedent for such action. Before George V would create the required number of Liberal peers to effect the passage of the Parliament Act 1911 he insisted upon the dissolution of Parliament and an election. This power is still vested in the monarch and it is correct to describe it as a personal prerogative rather than a conventional practice.

A more recent instance of this power of the monarch, and also the role of the monarch in appointing a PM, arose in Australia in 1975. The Governor-General of Australia represents the Queen and enjoys the power and privileges of the Head of State. As a result of an impasse between the House of Representatives and the Senate, the government was denied its financial support. In order to break the deadlock the Governor-General, Sir John Kerr, dismissed PM Gough Whitlam and called in the opposition leader as PM upon condition that he then requested a dissolution of Parliament. There would appear, however, to be no reason to suppose that the Governor-General, exercising the royal prerogative, could not insist upon a dissolution of Parliament.

The public conduct of the sovereign is largely determined by the operation of conventions. Although they are not laws, conventions are regarded by the sovereign as obligatory. Many matters, particularly relating to foreign affairs, such as the signing of treaties, are done in the name of the sovereign; they are not, however, associated with the public conduct of the sovereign. Those that are, such as the appointment of the Prime Minister, leave the sovereign with little discretion as to how to act. If an unpopular, in the eyes of Parliament, individual were to be appointed PM he or she would be unable to obtain a vote of confidence. It is the application of conventions that prevents the sovereign from becoming embroiled in political controversy and preserves the institution in a symbolic role.

References
(1) *Law of the Constitution* (10th edn, 1959)
(2) *The Law and the Constitution* (1959)
(3) On which see the Suggested Solution to Question 3
(4) See Question 3 for more details

QUESTION 3

Consider the view that 'our method of election to the House of Commons is in the highest degree unjust, unsatisfactory and dangerous'.

SUGGESTED SOLUTION TO QUESTION 3

General Comment

This question invites a discussion of the workings of the present electoral system. Candidates should discuss not only the present electoral system but also its consequences in the representation of the parties in Parliament. The advantages and disadvantages of the system should be set out and the student must be willing to agree or disagree with the polemical statement. A brief summary of some of the alternative electoral systems needs to be included to complete the essay.

Skeleton Solution

Introduction – the franchise in the UK.

Constituency basis of the MP.

'First Past the Post.'

The reflection of 'First Past the Post' in the Commons.

Advantages of the present system.

Disadvantages of the present system.

Alternative electoral systems.

Conclusion.

Suggested Solution

The membership of the House of Commons is elected on the basis of universal adult suffrage. In order to vote in a parliamentary election the individual must be listed in the electoral register for a parliamentary constituency. To be placed on the register the individual must be a British subject, a Commonwealth citizen or a citizen of the Irish Republic (such citizens are not classified as aliens for electoral purposes), be eighteen years of age or be due to attain his/her eighteenth birthday within twelve months of the publication of the register, not suffer any legal incapacity and be resident in the constituency on the qualifying date for compiling the register.

The above is without controversy and has raised little or no political discussion. It is the electoral system rather than those eligible to vote which is the cause of political disquiet, resulting in the Labour Party proposing, in 1996, to initiate a referendum, if they form the next government, on the electoral system.

How then is the electoral system to the House of Commons based? The United Kingdom is divided into 651 parliamentary constituencies, each of which is represented by one member in the House of Commons. The constituency boundaries are determined by the Boundary Commission which works on the theory that each constituency should have the same number of votes within it to ensure that all votes in the country are of equal value. This is summed up by the maxim: 'one man, one vote, one value'. The Boundary Commission reviews the electoral population of the parliamentary constituencies and may recommend that extra constituencies be formed in an area under-represented owing to an increase in population, or an abolition of constituencies owing to a decrease in population. These changes largely reflect the change in the balance of the population away from urban areas and into the shires. The Boundary Commission is not, however, obliged to reflect the voting population exclusively, as its terms of reference (Parliamentary Constituencies Act 1986) include the proviso that the number of constituencies in Scotland shall not be less than 71, a directive which results in the relative over-representation of Scotland at Westminister.

This division of the UK by the Boundary Commission is normally accepted by the political parties but its findings are still capable of judicial review, as the Court of Appeal accepted in their judgment in *R v Boundary Commission for England, ex parte Foot* (1).

Of much more controversy though is the electoral system. The UK system is categorised as 'First Past the Post'. Each elector is eligible to vote for one candidate only and the candidate who obtains the most votes within a constituency wins. It is possible, therefore, for a candidate to win even though the majority of the electorate in a constituency vote against him. If, for instance, J Bloggs obtains 10,000 votes, J Smith obtains 7,000 votes and J Jones obtains 6,000 votes, J Bloggs wins despite the fact the majority of the electorate voted against him. All the votes given to J Bloggs over 7,001 are 'wasted'. The number of wasted votes may be significant in a safe Labour seat, for example in South Wales, or in a safe Conservative seat, for instance in Surrey. There is no way in the existing system that the votes, or more accurately the surplus votes, may be distributed elsewhere in the country.

This system is reflected in the final outcome of the votes as there is litte relationship between the number of votes cast nationally for a party and the number of seats that party may obtain in the

House of Commons. Thus, in 1992 General Election the Conservatives obtained 41.9 per cent of the votes but achieved 51.6 per cent of the seats. Minority parties do particularly badly in this system, as illustrated by the Liberal Democrats who obtained 17.8 per cent of the votes in 1992 but only 3.1 per cent of the seats. As with racing, or even more so, there is little merit in coming second. Parties which come second in a significant number of constituencies, as with the Social Democratic Party in 1983, may as well have come third or fourth. The only minority parties likely to survive in such a system are those with a strong regional base, such as the Scottish Nationalists, or to some extent the Liberals in the 'celtic fringe'. They are able to target particular constituencies rather than have their votes spread out throughout the country.

It should be pointed out, however, that the 'First Past the Post' system has a number of advantages. It is simple and the electorate has a clear understanding of how it works. The results are easily arrived at and it avoids delays in establishing the winner on both a national and local level. It also establishes a link between the MP and his/her constituency; the other systems (see below) often fail to achieve this. The link between an MP and his/her constituency enables other institutions such as the Parliamentary Commissioner for Administration (PCA) to function effectively as the MP puts forward the complaints and grievances of the constituent. An MP may also pursue a particular matter which is of concern to his or her constituents. For example, Members of Parliament who have a large proportion of immigrants amongst their constituents are more likely to be involved in immigration issues. In taking up an issue raised by a constituent the MP is obliged to help the constituent to his or her best ability no matter whether the constituent is likely to vote for the MP or not.

A further advantage of the present system is that it usually creates an absolute (overall) majority of seats in the House of Commons. At the end of the day the electorate can understand the result of the election, while in other electoral systems (see below) this is not necessarily the case. The majority of British elections do not result in inter- and intra-party manoeuvres as a government is trying to be formed. A proportional representation system, with its possible result of a 'hung' Parliament, would also have the effect of politicising the role of the monarch as she would have to exercise her discretion as to which candidate would be the most suitable Prime Minister (2).

While it may be seen as unjust in the manner in which it penalises minority parties, the present electoral system does have the beneficial effect of preventing extremist minority parties obtaining a presence in the House of Commons. In the 1930s the British Fascist Party led by Oswald Mosley failed to obtain a seat in the House of Commons because its followers were spread throughout the country and the party failed to gain enough following to achieve a majority in a single constituency. Indeed, countries with a system of proportional representation, such as Germany, have a threshold requirement of about 5 per cent before a party can enter Parliament, the purpose being to prevent extremist minority parties gaining a platform.

What then are the alternatives to the British electoral system? The main options are these systems:

a) alternative vote;
b) party list; and
c) single transferable vote.

The alternative vote system operates by the voter listing the candidates in their constituency in order of preference. If no candidate gains an absolute majority of the first preference then the lowest candidate is eliminated and his/her second preference votes are distributed amongst the other candidates. This process can be repeated until one candidate emerges with an absolute majority. The principal inadequacy of the system is that the overall result does not reflect the actual proportions of the votes. The voter has the potential to be confused with the procedure and the winner might not have a clear mandate from the voters.

The party list system is perhaps the method which best reflects the real proportion of the votes. The country is classified as one constituency and the parties present lists of candidates and the electors vote for the whole party list. Seats in Parliament are allocated to the parties in proportion to the votes received by each party list. Such a system strengthens the party bureaucracy as potential candidates compete to be placed as near the top of the list as possible. The link between the MP and the constituency is destroyed and minority parties will be given greater potential power as they offer their conditional support to any putative government. This effect is increased as an outright winner in such a system is unusual.

The single transferable vote (STV) is the system which is looked upon with most approval by the advocates of electoral reform. This system would see a diminution in the number of constituencies in Parliament, as it requires multi-member constituencies with between five and seven members. Voters list the candidates in order of preference. The candidate needs a quota of votes to be elected. The 'surplus' votes of the winning candidate are then redistributed among the other candidates in accordance with the voter's second preference. While this system would weaken the link between the MP and his constituents it is not unknown in the UK. In the nineteenth century multi-member constituencies (usually two MPs) were present in the UK Parliament.

The call for reform of the electoral system in the UK is heard especially from those parties such as the Liberals (and the former SDP) who are penalised by being minority parties. There is no manner in which their votes may be distributed. The Labour Party, or sections of it, frustrated after 17 years in opposition, is also flirting with the idea of electoral reform. Unfortunately, the debate is often centred on the economic and social success of a particular country. The advocates of electoral reform point to the German voting system while the detractors point to Israel or Ireland. The message elsewhere is unclear; while New Zealand has introduced a system of proportional representation, Italy has moved away from it. One might conclude that our method of election is unjust and unsatisfactory, but so are all the others.

References
(1)   [1983] QB 600
(2)   See the Suggested Solution to Question 2 for a further discussion

QUESTION 4

Discuss, by reference to decided cases, the legal status of European Community law within the United Kingdom and its priority in relation to provisions in domestic Acts of Parliament.

SUGGESTED SOLUTION TO QUESTION 4

General Comment
This is a relatively straightforward question involving the case law relating to the UK's membership of the European Community. The candidate should highlight the leading cases in this area and avoid getting enmeshed in a descriptive analysis of the plethora of cases in this area.

A detailed knowledge, inter alia, of the course and implications of the *Factortame* litigation is required.

Skeleton Solution
UK's membership of the EU and the method by which treaties are signed.

Implications for domestic law of the signing of treaties.

Sections 2(1), 2(4) and 3 European Communities Act 1972.

Question of express and implied repeal.

McCarthys v *Smith*.

Factortame cases – art 177.

How the EU sees itself and conclusion.

Suggested Solution
The United Kingdom as an international legal personality joined the European Economic Community (as it then was) by the act of signing and ratifying the Treaty of Rome under the power vested in the royal prerogative. This was not as such a departure from previous practice dealing with treaties. The power so to do cannot be impugned or questioned in the courts (*Blackburn* v *Attorney-General* (1)). The royal prerogative is not, however, capable of enacting new laws and, as the *Case of Proclamations* (2) established, the Crown is unable to make new prerogative powers or laws imposing rights or obligations upon the Crown's subjects. Therefore, in order to give domestic effect to the Treaty of Rome it was necessary to incorporate the Treaty into UK municipal law. This was done by the enactment of the European Communities Act 1972. The terms of the statute are far-reaching. By s2(1) both

primary – the Treaty – and secondary Community law is to be given legal effect in the UK.

This applies to Community law past, present and future. Moreover, under s3 of the statute the interpretation of Community treaties and legislation is regarded as a question of law to be interpreted either by the European Court of Justice at Luxembourg (ECJ) or, if it is decided by the courts of the UK, the matter is to be decided in accordance with ECJ decisions. The wording of s2(4) presents the UK courts with the dilemma of how to interpret Community law and subsequent Acts of Parliament, stating that: 'any existing or future enactments are to be construed and have effect subject to the foregoing provisions of this section'.

This would appear to be constitutional nonsense. According to the traditional doctrine of parliamentary sovereignty one Parliament cannot bind future Parliaments. Sovereignty is continuing and one Parliament cannot see itself up as being superior to any future Parliament or Parliaments. A subsequent Act of Parliament may expressly or impliedly repeal any previous legislation. English case law contains a plethora of decisions substantiating the above proposition. In the case of *Ellen Street Estates Ltd* v *Minister of Health* (3) Maugham LJ held, inter alia:

> 'If in a subsequent Act, Parliament chooses to make it plain that the earlier statute is being to some extent repealed, effect must be given to that intention just because it is the will of the legislature.'

Such is, or was, the theory. In the case of *Blackburn* v *Attorney-General* Lord Denning chose to cast doubt on the orthodox theory and its relation to reality. Speaking obiter he said:

> 'We have all been brought up to believe that in legal theory one Parliament cannot bind another and that no Act is irreversible. But legal theory does not always march alongside political reality.'

He then went on to discuss the unlikely instance of Parliament reversing an Act of independence to a former colony, arguing 'Freedom once given cannot be taken away. Legal theory must give way to practical politics.'

What then is the position with relation to European Union law and any conflicting Acts of Parliament? In the case of *Macarthys Ltd* v *Smith* (4) Lord Denning again turned his attention to this problem. Speaking obiter he hypothesised:

> 'Thus far I have assumed that our Parliament whenever it passes legislation intends to fulfil its obligations under the Treaty. If the time should come when our Parliament *deliberately passes an Act* – with the intention of repudiating the Treaty or any provision in it – or intentionally acting inconsistently with it – and says so in express terms – then I should have thought that it would be the duty of our

courts to follow the statute of our Parliament. I do not, however, envisage any such situation.'

Thus Lord Denning is acknowledging that if Parliament intends to repudiate Community law (as it then was), then the UK courts will give effect to it. However, one should be aware and pay attention to the phrase used: 'express terms'. It is submitted that this is less than express repeal and an implied repeal may be in express terms.

In his judgment Lord Denning also provides for an escape clause from any possible conflict by talking about 'some oversight of our draftsmen' when a conflict with Community law is apparent. So what is 'express terms' or what is 'an oversight of our draftsmen' is conveniently left to the UK courts to interpret.

Another aspect of the potential conflict between the two jurisdictions which the courts have had to tackle arises when there is a *perceived* conflict between the UK law and EU law. This is discussed in the series of *Factortame* cases.

The Common Market Fishing Policy devised a system to conserve fish by fixing quotas for national fishing fleets. The British government established a licensing system in 1985, which was expanded upon in the Merchant Shipping Act 1988 and which empowered the Secretary for Transport to make regulations and introduce a new register of British fishing vessels designed to prevent so-called 'quota hopping', whereby non-British Community nationals, Spanish fishermen, established companies in the UK in order to avail themselves of the British fishing quota. The question which arose before the UK courts was if a UK Act of Parliament supposedly infringed a party's Community rights – in this case as a result of discrimination based on the grounds of nationality – could that Act could be suspended pending a final outcome? The House of Lords (5) initially answered 'no' but referred the case to the ECJ, under art 177, for a preliminary ruling. The UK courts will avail themselves of art 177 when, inter alia, a question of interpretation of Community law needs to be answered (6).

The ECJ in its preliminary ruling argued that the full effectiveness of Community law would be impaired if the UK argument that they could not suspend an Act of Parliament in such circumstances were to prevail. The ECJ (7) argued that, pending a final outcome, interim relief should be granted and the House of Lords (8) granted the said relief. A temporary injunction was issued against the Secretary of State preventing him from enforcing the offending provisions of the statute. Injunctive relief was therefore granted against the Crown and an Act of Parliament was suspended. In *Factortame (No 3)* (9) the ruling of the ECJ upheld the complaints of the Spanish fishermen. Therefore, for the first time in UK constitutional history an Act of Parliament was suspended upon the basis of a violation of alleged rights, never mind established rights, and injunctive relief was given against the Crown.

The legal revolution as a result of joining the European Community has also been commented upon in other areas of litigation. Hoffman J (as he then was) put it succinctly:

'The EC Treaty is the supreme law of this country, taking precedent over Acts of Parliament. Our entry into the EC meant that Parliament surrendered its sovereign right to legislate contrary to the provisions of the Treaty on matters of social and economic policy which it regulated' (10).

Whether or not the courts of the UK would disallow an Act of Parliament if it were to say 'notwithstanding EU law to the contrary' such and such is to apply is an open question. As it is the UK Courts have clearly absorbed the philosophy of the ECJ in *Costa v ENEL* (11), when it argued in effect that a new legal order had been created. The UK courts will now not only suspend the workings of a statute but will also entertain an application for judicial review from, for example, the Equal Opportunities Commission (12) for a declaration that UK law is incompatible with Community law. It is indeed true to say, as Lord Denning stated in *Bulmer v Bollinger* (13), that 'the Treaty [ie the Treaty of Rome] is like an incoming tide. It flows into the estuaries and up the rivers. It cannot be held back'.

References

(1) *Blackburn v Attorney-General* [1971] 2 All ER 1380
(2) (1611) 12 Co Rep 74
(3) [1934] 1 KB 590
(4) [1979] 3 CMLR 44
(5) *R v Secretary of State for Transport, ex parte Factortame* [1989] 2 WLR 997
(6) *Bulmer Ltd v Bollinger* [1974] 3 WLR 202; see also *Customs and Exercise Commissioners v APS Samex* [1983] 1 All ER 1042
(7) Case 213/89 [1990] ECR 2433
(8) [1991] 3 WLR 818
(9) [1991] 3 All ER 769
(10) *Stoke-on-Trent City Council v B & Q plc* [1991] 2 WLR 42 at 45
(11) [1964] CMLR 425
(12) *R v Secretary of State for Employment, ex parte Equal Opportunities Commission* (1994) The Times 4 March
(13) [1974] Ch 401

QUESTION 5

Article 11 of the European Convention on Human Rights provides that 'Everyone has the right to peaceful assembly'. How is this human right guaranteed in English Law?

SUGGESTED SOLUTION TO QUESTION 5

General Comment

This is a potentially wide-ranging question and the student should direct his/her attention to the area of assemblies and not be diverted into discussing other areas of public order such as processions. The main statutes to be familiar with are the relevant sections of the Public Order Act 1986 and the Criminal Justice and Public Order Act 1994. In addition, candidates should be aware of the available common law powers to curb an assembly, as well as any statutes which might be utilised for this purpose.

Skeleton Solution

The issue of 'rights' in English law.

Section 14 Public Order Act (POA) 1986.

Criminal Justice and Public Order Act (CJPOA) 1994 – trespass, trespassary assemblies, 'raves'.

Common law powers to control assemblies.

Highways Act 1980.

Conclusion.

Suggested Solution

English law does not, of course, recognise any rights on a positive attribute. According to Dicey (1), rights are regarded as residual. This means that the individual is permitted to do something provided it is not forbidden. When one examines the law relating to peaceful assembly this necessarily entails an analysis of the restrictions which may be imposed on individuals or groups. The restrictions in this area take the form of statutory and common law curtailments on freedom of assembly.

Unlike the law relating to processions, the Public Order Act (POA) 1986 imposes no requirement to obtain permission from the police in order to organise an assembly. A public assembly is defined by s16 POA 1986 as being 'an assembly of 20 or more persons in a public place which is wholly or partly open to the air'.

While, however, no permission is needed to organise an

assembly it has to be in the words of art 11 a 'peaceful' gathering. If a senior police officer reasonably believes that the assembly will result in serious public disorder, serious damage to property or serious disruption to the life of the community, or the purpose is the intimidation of others (2), he may impose conditions on the organisers relating to the duration of the assembly and the maximum number of people who may make up the meeting: s14 POA 1986. What constitutes the reasonable belief of the senior police officer (presumably the senior police officer present) as to these factors is not defined in the Act. One may suppose that the belief is either '*Wednesbury* reasonableness' (3), or more likely a combination of subjective/objective reasonableness. That is, did the police officer have an honest and reasonable belief as to the facts and would a police officer in those circumstances have reasonably formed this view? What is certain is that a police officer cannot arbitrarily forbid an assembly.

A much more far-reaching statute in this area is the Criminal Justice and Public Order Act (CJPOA) 1994. This Act was passed in response to a number of public order issues ranging from 'New Age Travellers' to 'rave' parties on disused airfields. Associated with these groups and events is the issue of trespass and trespassary assembly. The POA 1986 attempted to deal with some of these issues by providing a senior police officer (ie the most senior present) with powers to direct trespassers to leave land: s39 POA 1986. These could only be invoked if the police officer believed that two or more persons had entered the land as trespassers with a common purpose of residing there, that they had not heeded reasonable steps, by the occupier, to leave and that they had caused damage to the property on the land or that they had used threatening, abusive or insulting words or behaviour towards the occupier or his agent. The police officer could also direct the trespassers to leave the land if they brought 12 or more vehicles on the land: s39(1)(b).

The above proved inadequate to deal with a number of increasingly popular gatherings in the 1980s and 90s. Section 61 CJPOA 1994 went further than s39 POA 1986. By s61, even in the case of individuals who entered the land by invitation, if the invitation is withdrawn they are then categorised as trespassers and can be asked to leave. Moreover, while s39 talked about damage to property, the CJPOA talks about damage to the land. Damage may presumably be caused by cars driving onto fields and the number of vehicles has been reduced from 12 or more (in s39) to six. The use of the definition of land has now been extended and, for instance, common land and bridleways are included.

Gatherings at historical monuments may also be curtailed, a move designed to prevent the gathering of people at the time of the summer solstice at Stonehenge. By s70 CJPOA 1994 the relevant chief police officer may apply to the local council for an order prohibiting for a specified period the holding of all trespassary public assemblies in a specified area, provided the Secretary of State consents. One of the specified areas described in the statute is an area of historical monuments, provided that a case is made out of potential damage to the said structures.

Assemblies may also be prohibited if their aim is to disrupt or obstruct a lawful activity by trespassing on land in the open air with that aim in mind. This new offence of 'aggravated trespass' (s68(1)) is designed to include the activities of, for instance, hunt saboteurs.

Finally, the CJPOA has prohibited assemblies in the open air where amplified music is played during the night, provided there is an attendance of 100 or more people: s63. Moreover, the Act gives the police a new power to stop somebody they reasonably believe is travelling to such an assembly or 'rave'. This power can only be utilised within five miles of the boundary of the assembly: s65.

In addition, English law has extensive common law powers which in effect curtail an assembly. The test is whether there will be a breach of the peace or a reasonable likelihood of breach of the peace at the gathering, rather than what is the intention of the organisers or those attempting to reach the assembly. In *O'Kelly* v *Harvey* (4), for instance, a meeting of the 'Land League' was ordered to be dispersed by the local justice of the peace as it was in danger of being broken up 'Orangemen' – members of a Protestant organisation hostile to the aspirations of the Land League. The reasoning of this nineteenth-century precedent has been utilised by the police in preventing individuals from attending a gathering whose purpose is per se lawful. In *Moss* v *McLachlan* (5) the Divisional Court held that the police had reasonable grounds for apprehending a breach of the peace as imminent when they stopped a group of striking miners from going to attend a mass picket. The miners were arrested for obstruction of the police. It is not necessary in such a situation to argue that the meeting is unlawful, but rather whether the natural consequence of the meeting will be a breach of the peace. If, however, the natural consequence of an assembly is not to provoke violence then it would appear that it is legitimate to proceed. *R* v *Morpeth Ward Justices, ex parte Ward and Others* (6) appears to indicate that individuals may protest at a meeting but not in a manner likely to provoke violence. Such reasoning is an echo of

Beatty v *Gillbanks* (7) in which the court emphasised that so long as the participants at a gathering were 'quiet and reasonable' then the unlawful actions of the other participants were not deemed to be the 'natural consequences' of the event.

Further to the above, a peaceful assembly may fall foul of additional legislation which may have been passed with other situations in mind. The Highways Act 1980 is a piece of legislation which falls into this category. Designed to provide for free passage along the highway it has also been utilised to curb demonstrations and assemblies – from an attempt to halt a demonstration outside a fur shop (*Hirst* v *Chief Constable for West Yorkshire* (8)) (reversed on appeal) to the arrest for obstruction of the highway of the television presenter Esther Rantzen for stopping pedestrians and asking them to sample bat soup!

In conclusion, the individual may attend a peaceful assembly but the constraints are numerous. Legislation has been passed in response to such phenomenon as New Age Travellers and rave parties; in their desire to preserve public order statute and common law have limited the opportunity to convene an assembly.

References

(1)   Dicey, *Law of the Constitution* (10th edn, 1959)
(2)   See *Police* v *Reid* [1987] Crim LR 702
(3)   *Associated Provincial Picture Houses Ltd* v *Wednesbury Corporation* [1948] 1 KB 223 and see the discussion in Question 8 for a definition of this term
(4)   (1883) 15 Cox CC 435
(5)   [1985] IRLR 76
(6)   [1992] Crim LR 497
(7)   (1882) 9 QB 308
(8)   (1987) 85 Cr App R 143

QUESTION 6

Compare and contrast the effectiveness of judicial and parliamentary controls over the exercise of prerogative executive powers by government ministers.

SUGGESTED SOLUTION TO QUESTION 6

General Comment

The question involves a detailed discussion of the cases involved in examining the exercise of the prerogative. Candidates should be familiar with the decision of the House of Lords in the so-called GCHQ case and its potential as revealed in subsequent cases.

With reference to parliamentary control in this area some of the knowledge in relation to the role of the Attorney-General (covered in depth in the answer to Question 1) may be utilised. Candidates should be familiar with the operation of the prerogative in foreign affairs (acts of State) and how these are or are not controlled by Parliament.

Skeleton Solution

Definition of royal prerogative.

Who exercises it?

The attitude of the courts to its exercise: *Council of Civil Service Unions v Minister for the Civil Service.*

Ex parte Everett

Ex parte Bentley

Prerogative and statutory authority.

Parliamentary control.

The role of the Attorney-General.

The prerogative in foreign affairs.

Conclusion.

Suggested Solution

The royal prerogative consists of those powers which are unique and inherent to the Crown. These powers are in the majority of cases exercised by the Crown in an executive capacity, by which is meant the government. The prerogative is a non-statutory power which may be described as having a common law source, or recognised by the common law. Its extent is finite and since the seventeenth century it is clear from judicial pronouncements that it cannot be extended. In the words of Lord Diplock in *BBC* v *Johns* (1):

> 'It is 350 years and a civil war too late for the Queen's courts to broaden the prerogative.'

The seminal case which defined the attitude of the courts to the attempt by the Crown to extend the prerogative is the *Case of Proclamations* (2). James I sought to create a new offence without seeking parliamentary approval. The court was robust in quashing such a use or misuse of the prerogative. Coke CJ held that: 'the King hath no prerogative, but that which the law of the land allows him'.

Since the *Case of Proclamations* it has become clear that the Crown cannot create a new offence or in other ways punish its subjects except by an Act of Parliament.

The seventeenth-century pronouncement by Coke CJ in relation to the courts determining the extent of the prerogative has survived intact, and if the British Constitution has any fundamentals then this might be one of them. It was not, however, until relatively recently that the courts felt confident enough to challenge the exercise of the prerogative by the executive. Dicey (3) argued that the prerogative may be seen as an arbitrary power in the sense that once the courts have determined its existence they will no longer utilise their jurisdictional powers to examine the adequacy of the grounds upon which it has been exercised. A change in judicial attitudes was foreshadowed by Lord Denning in *Laker Airways* v *Department of Trade* (4) and was expanded upon by the House of Lords in the leading case of *Council of Civil Service Unions* v *Minister for the Civil Service* (5).

This latter case centres around the government intelligence institution known as GCHQ, a public service institution under the Foreign and Commonwealth Office. As a result of civil service industrial action the government, acting under an Order in Council issued by virtue of the prerogative, sought to ban trade union membership for those working at the institution. This was done without any prior consultation. The prerogative power involved was the power to regulate the Home Civil Service.

The House of Lords was presented with the question as to whether the exercise of the prerogative could be examined in the courts. The Lords answered in the affirmative though this did not apply to all the prerogative powers and not under all circumstances. Lord Diplock held that judicial review had developed to a stage where one could classify under three heads the grounds upon which administrative action was subject to control by judicial review: (a) illegality; (b) irrationality; and (c) procedural impropriety. There was in this case procedural impropriety as the unions had not been consulted before the ban was imposed. Their Lordships were, however, agreed, following earlier precedents, that procedural impropriety must give way to national security.

The importance of the case lies not, however, upon its particular facts but rather its potential. The House of Lords was unanimous in holding that the prerogative is capable of judicial review in its exercise; the difference of opinion centred around how the courts were to determine which prerogatives were so capable. Lord Scarman emphasised the subject matter, while Lord Roskill argued that certain prerogatives, such as the making of treaties and the defence of the realm, were not in their nature amenable to judicial review.

The decision in the GCHQ case has been followed by other judgments, for example, rendering the issuance or non-issuance of passports subject to judicial review (*R v Secretary of State for Foreign and Commonwealth Affairs, ex parte Everett* (6)), and even a willingness to urge the Home Secretary to 'think again' in his refusal to exercise his prerogative of pardon (*R v Secretary of State for the Home Department, ex parte Bentley* (7)). Nor will the courts refrain from holding a minister of the Crown to be personally liable in his official capacity for contempt of court: *M v Home Office* (8).

The courts have also been active in examining the relationship between the prerogative and statutes as a source of power. In *Attorney-General v De Keyser's Royal Hotel Ltd* (9) the House of Lords emphasised that the courts will not permit the use of the prerogative when a statute covers the same area. The Crown is obliged to use the statute even if the terms are less advantageous to it. What exactly happens to the prerogatives in these circumstances is unclear, but Lord Atkinson was of the opinion that the prerogative went into abeyance. A statute may of course abolish the prerogative, as with the Crown Proceedings Act 1947, rather than just covering the same area. The case of *De Keyser's Royal Hotel* presumes that the Crown has a monopoly of power. In an area where this is not the case, the Court of Appeal has been willing (*Secretary of State for the Home Department, ex parte Northumbria Police Authority* (10)) to hold that a statutory power and a prerogative power may co-exist covering the same subject matter (the issuance of riot gear to the police) but only where they are exercised by separate bodies – the police authority and the Home Secretary.

The courts have taken a more robust attitude when discussing this relationship in other areas. In *R v Secretary of State for the Home*

Department, ex parte Fire Brigades Union (11), the Home Secretary had attempted to use the prerogative to amend the workings of the Criminal Injuries Compensation Scheme, which had itself been set up under the royal prerogative. By a majority the House of Lords ruled that this was unlawful. There was an alternative scheme from the Criminal Justice Act 1988 already on the statue book (but not yet in force), and the Home Secretary could neither abuse his power to introduce that by deciding never to do so, nor could he frustrate the will of Parliament by introducing a scheme so different to that which they had approved.

Parliamentary control over the governmental exercise of the prerogative varies in effectiveness depending upon the subject matter. As has been mentioned, the signing of treaties is a prerogative act and whether they are ever discussed or approved by Parliament often depends upon the will of the executive. If, however, a treaty is to have domestic effect (as with European Community and Union treaties), then an Act of Parliament must be passed. A declaration of war is also a prerogative power and, for instance, the declaration of war against Germany in 1939 was carried out without parliamentary approval. The Crown does not, however, have any independent source of revenue, and if Parliament were to oppose the military action then the government would run out of money.

Individual office holders in the exercise of their prerogative functions are not in some cases answerable to the courts but are answerable to Parliament. The Attorney-General in performing his role as a quasi-judicial officer of the Crown is not answerable to the courts (12), but *is* answerable to Parliament, and theoretically could be asked to resign after a vote of no confidence. Similarly, moves by the court notwithstanding (13), the Home Secretary is answerable to Parliament for his acts or omissions in not granting a prerogative of mercy or pardon.

The above is, of course, dependent upon the workings of the House of Commons, and if the government of the day can maintain a majority in any vote of confidence then the office holder will survive. Other prerogatives, such as the granting of honours, are not open to parliamentary scrutiny nor any prerogative functions involving defence of the realm.

One may conclude that while the courts are now robust in examining the prerogative, and more particularly its exercise, parliamentary control is hindered by the impact of the party system upon the workings of the House of Commons in particular. There is a word of warning, though. One should not draw far-reaching conclusions from particular events. On the facts of the

GCHQ case the trade unions failed in their case but the potential of the House of Lords' decision was there for all to see. Similarly, the perceived weakness of Parliament in controlling the prerogative exercise by ministers could be reversed if minority governments were to become the norm rather than the exception.

References

(1) [1965] Ch 32
(2) (1611) 12 Co Rep 74
(3) *Law of the Constitution* (10th edn, 1959)
(4) [1976] 3 WLR 537
(5) [1984] 3 WLR 1174
(6) [1989] 1 All ER 655
(7) [1994] 4 All ER 442
(8) [1993] 3 WLR 433
(9) [1920] AC 508
(10) [1988] 1 All ER 556
(11) [1995] 2 WLR 1
(12) See the discussion in the Suggested Solution to Question 1
(13) See the discussion of *ex parte Bentley* above

QUESTION 7

Discuss the range of legal powers by which central government controls the actions of local authorities.

SUGGESTED SOLUTION TO QUESTION 7

General Comment

This is a relatively straightforward question which requires an understanding of the miscellany of statutory enactments controlling the operation of local government.

An understanding of the nature of local government in the constitution and how local authorities obtain their status and power is necessary. The candidate should be aware of a selection of administrative law cases dealing with the enactments of local authorities and how these relate to statutory controls. In addition a brief summary of local government expenditure, revenue raising and functions is necessary.

Skeleton Solution

Introduction: status of local government.

Administrative interpretation of local government actions – fiduciary relationship – relator actions.

Revenue raising and local government.

Expenditure of local government.

Examples of local government functions, eg education.

Conclusion.

Suggested Solution

Local authorities in the UK have only a derivative power. In the unifed constitution of the UK local government may be reorganised, as with Local Government Act 1972, or they may be abolished as with the case of the Greater London Council. Local government may only perform those tasks which the Parliament at Westminister permits it to carry out. Local authorities may, of course, enact legislation (bye-laws), but these are by their nature delegated legislation and must conform to the terms and conditions laid down by the 'parent Act'. If they fail to do so then the courts will hold the bye-laws ultra vires. In addition, any bye-law passed is subject to confirmation by the appropriate minister. The width of the 'parent Act' is something for the Westminister

49

Parliment to decide, and if the statute is narrowly drawn then the powers of the local authority will be curtailed.

The ambit of the parent Act is in the final analysis determined by the courts, and it is often in such situations that the judiciary has been more active in controlling the actions of local government than the central government might have wished. *R v Greater London Council, ex parte Bromley London Borough* (1) may serve to illustrate this proposition. The Greater London Council in its 'fares fair' policy decided to reduce bus and tube fares by 25 per cent. This was attacked, inter alia, on the basis that it ran contrary to the Transport (London) Act 1969. Section 1 of the statute stated that the general duty of the GLC was 'to develop and encourage measures which would promote the provision of integrated efficient and economic transport facilities and services for Greater London'. Some of their Lordships based their argument upon the phrase 'efficient and economic'. Lord Wilberforce, for instance, argued that economic meant 'cost effective'. A subsidy to the transport network, at the expense of the ratepayer, was held to violate the terms of the legislation. Upon this and other arguments (see below) the transport policy of the GLC was declared ultra vires. It remains open to interpretation whether the wording of the Transport Act was an attempt to control the actions of the GLC, or whether the case illustrates an unduly restrictive approach by the judiciary.

A similar controversy has arisen over the courts' introduction of the equitable concept of the fiduciary relationship to the area of local government taxation and expenditure. In *Prescott v Birmingham Corporation* (2) the court held that local authorities owed a fiduciary duty, analogous to that of a trustee, to their ratepayers. Therefore, although a body having statutory power to charge tolls was given a discretionary power by the relevant statutes, the local authority was not entitled to make a gift of free travel (for 'Senior Citizens') at the expense of the ratepayer. It was also implied, as with the *GLC* case, that the transport undertaking of Birmingham Corporation should be run as a business venture. Lord Diplock also took up the 'fiduciary' line of argument in the *GLC* case, as the effect of the GLC's policy on fares would result in the loss of the central government's rate support grant and increase the burden on the ratepayers.

In addition to the above, the courts have also implied the use of the word 'reasonable' in interpreting a statutory power given to a local authority, an interpretation which has excited controversy since the case of *Roberts v Hopwood* (3). This case was concerned with s62 Metropolitan Management Act 1855, by which a metropolitan borough council was entitled to employ 'such servants as may be necessary and may allow to such servants *such wages as [the Council] may think fit'* (emphasis added).

From these supposedly open-ended words the House of Lords held that the council's power must be exercised reasonably, and as the council had fixed the wages of its employees without relation to the market conditions prevailing at the time, this was unreasonable. The question of how to determine what is reasonable or not was expanded upon a decade later in the *Wednesbury* case (4). Whether it is correct to classify these examples of litigation as being judicial interpretation of parliamentary intentions or a judicial creativity is open to question. Writers such as JAG Griffith (5) would adhere to the latter view.

If the Attorney-General is of the opinion that the local government has exceeded its powers it is always open to him to commence litigation by way of a relator action. Such a procedure cannot, however, be classified as central government control of a local authority, as the Attorney-General is not acting in his capacity as a government minister but rather as a quasi-judicial officer of the Crown (6).

All the above involve indirect control over local authorities. A symptom of the past seventeen years of Conservative power is the increase in direct control from central government. Local government finance is one of the keys, if not the main one, to understanding the degree of control involved. As local government only raises about 40 per cent of its revenue, it is dependent upon central government for the remainder. It has limited powers of borrowing, which are controlled by the central government.

Local authorities now raise revenue by means of the council tax (introduced in 1993). Edmund Burke opined that 'to tax and to please is not given to man' and is particularly true of local government taxation. The council tax was introduced after the widespread unpopularity of the community charge, which was known as the 'poll tax'. The present system is formulated on the value of the property within different price bands.

Local authorities are instructed how to raise revenue and they are not free to spend it as they think fit. 'Rate capping' was introduced by the Rates Act 1984. Once a local authority exceeds its target as determined by central government, then the Secretary of State has the power to enact sanctions against the erring council.

In the area of eduction central government has been eroding the autonomy of local councils since the mid-nineteenth century, but it has recently gained momentum, particularly in the last decade. The Education Reform Act 1988 gives the central government control over the national curriculum and the methods of assessment. While not quite similar to the gibe about the French Minister of Education knowing exactly what is being taught at a particular hour of the day, it is nevertheless a symptom of national control. Also the management of schools may be transferred from the local authorities to the schools' governors provided the minister agrees, with the funding coming from central government. The Education Act also introduced city technology colleges which are set up by the Secretary of State for Education and are recipients of private funding.

Thus, it can be seen that in a variety of ways, from the diminution of local government control over education to the imposition of local government expenditure controls, local authorities are subject to the whim of central government. They do not exist in their own right and their activities may be curtailed by the enactment of government legislation. With the present structure of the British constitution such an outcome is inevitable, the only subject of discussion is the amount of central government control. The fact that local authorities may be subject to an audit (7), and that the Secretary of State may direct an audit to examine the efficiency and effectiveness of local authority expenditure, vividly illustrates this point.

References

(1) [1982] 2 WLR 62
(2) [1955] Ch 210
(3) [1925] AC 578
(4) *Associated Provincial Picture Houses Ltd* v *Wednesbury Corporation* [1948] 1 KB 223 and see the Suggested Solution to Question 8
(5) *The Politics of the Judiciary* (4th edn, 1991)
(6) See the Suggested Solution to Question 1 for a discussion on the role of the Attorney-General
(7) Local Government Finance Act 1982

QUESTION 8

Section 2 of the (fictitious) National Health Act 1996, provides that Area Health Authorities 'are under a duty to maintain adequate hospital beds and services to ensure the protection and maintenance of the health of residents in the area'.

In January 1996, the (fictitious) Western Area Health Authority, in an effort to cut costs, decided to close two hospital wards usually reserved for elderly patients requiring long-term care, and a ward containing ten beds reserved for patients in need of either pre- or post-operative intensive care.

In April 1996, Mrs Jones, who is elderly and has no living relatives to care for her, was admitted to the Wellbeing Hospital, a national health service hospital in the Western area. In June, however, Mr Smith, a hospital administrator, notified Mrs Jones that she would have to leave hospital within a week, even though she could not care for herself.

In February 1996, Toby, who is six years old, was found to be suffering from a rare bone marrow disease. The Wellbeing Hospital has refused to admit Toby for urgent surgery because of the shortage of beds. His mother, Mrs Jones, has been told that he will have to wait 'for up to three months' for the necessary surgery. She has consulted another doctor, who is a family friend, who has advised her that the delay in treatment could seriously affect Toby's chances of a full recovery from the disease.

Advise Mrs Brown and Mrs Jones as to whether they are entitled to seek a remedy by way of an action for judicial review, and as to the likely outcome of any judicial review proceedings.

SUGGESTED SOLUTION TO QUESTION 8

General Comment
This question involves judicial review. There are a number of issues present in the problem and the candidate should be aware of substantive administrative law and the procedure necessary to obtain a judicial review of an administrative action. The subject necessary involves a consideration of a significant amount of case law. It is normally not necessary nor desirable to examine the facts of the cases.

In the problem there is an obvious misprint. To make sense of the question, Mrs Jones in the fourth paragraph should be Mrs Brown. The writer of the Suggested Solution has made this assumption.

Skeleton Solution
'Sufficient interest'
Basis of the claim of Mrs Jones:
– statutory interpretation, illegality;
– irrelevant considerations;
– ignoring relevant considerations;
– unlawful delegation;
– procedural impropriety;
– fettering of discretion.
Basis of the claim of Mrs Brown
– breach of statutory duty;
– unlawful delegation;
– *Wednesbury* unreasonableness;
– public law and the remedies available.

Suggested Solution
The first matter to consider in advising Mrs Brown and Mrs Jones is whether they have sufficient interest to bring an action for judicial review. The Supreme Court Act (SCA) 1981 states that the

court will not grant leave for an application for judicial review unless the applicant has 'sufficient interest' or locus standi, ie the applicant must have an interest in the matter for which the application is being made. This is described in *R v Inland Revenue Commissioners, ex parte National Federation of Self-Employed and Small Businesses* (1), as 'an interest over and above that of the general public', a categorisation which the courts have expanded and been flexible in determining. Locus standi is determined at two stages of judicial review proceedings. First, when leave to apply is sought and, second, when the court examines the merits of the case (see eg *R v Oxford, ex parte Levey* (2)).

In the present case Mrs Brown would appear to have sufficient interest as she is the mother of Toby. The courts are relatively pragmatic in defining locus standi and, as Lord Diplock argued in the *National Federation* case, there is considerable room for evaluation of this concept. There was a clear demonstration of this in *R v IBA, ex parte Whitehouse* (3) in which the Divisional Court was prepared to grant Mary Whitehouse locus standi in her attempt to review a decision of the Independent Broadcasting Authority (IBA), on the ground that she was a sole licence holder. In cases involving a matter of public concern the courts are prepared to be open to suggestion with relation to locus standi. In the present instance the attempt to ration surgical care is of obvious public interest and the mother is likely to obtain leave to bring the case.

As to Mrs Jones, the courts are also likely to grant her leave as she is certainly going to suffer if she is dismissed from the hospital.

Having established that the two individuals may seek a judicial review upon the basis of their standing, upon what grounds may they challenge their respective decisions?

First, we turn to consider the case of Mrs Jones. She is told that she must leave the hospital within a week even though she is unable to care for herself. Section 2 of the (fictitious) statute states that health authorities 'are under a duty to maintain adequate hospital beds and services and to ensure the protection and maintenance of the health of the residents in the area'. The reasons of the Western Area Health Authority cannot be reconciled with the intent and purposes of the statute, an outcome which will render their decision ultra vires: *Padfield v Minister for Agriculture* (4). They are discharging Mrs Jones in an attempt to cut costs, which is not reconcilable with the statute and is in breach of their duty to maintain adequate hospital beds. If an authority is under a duty to act, which the Western Area Health Authority is, then failure to act may be classified as unlawful. This area is, however, more problematical as it involves questions of public policy and inadequacy of resources. The courts are reluctant to act if the matter involves a difference of opinion over the allocation of resources or the merits of a case (5).

A more fertile avenue for Mrs Jones to explore is that the Health Authority has fail to take into account the relevant consideration that Mrs Jones cannot care for herself and she is unable to call upon any relatives to help her. In the case of *Roberts v Hopwood* (5) the House of Lords held that failure to do such a thing would render a decision ultra vires and unreasonable. Similarly, the House of Lords so held in *R v Greater London Council, ex parte Bromley London Borough Council* (6).

Closely related to the above is the exercise of a discretion for an irrelevant purpose, in this case to save money. In the case of *Roberts v Hopwood* the irrelevant purpose was to act as a model socialist employer and in the *GLC* case to advance the benefits of public transport. In this instance it is to save money, although the courts would be reluctant to trespass into such controversial political area.

Mrs Jones might have some chance of success if she argued that the Health Authority was acting with an improper purpose. Powers must be used for the purpose for which they are granted: see eg: *Congreve v Home Office* (7). In this case the improper purpose is to cut costs. Improper purpose is a less onerous test than bad faith, which implies dishonesty and something which is more grave than taking into account irrelevant considerations: *Cannock Chase District Council v Kelly* (8).

Mrs Jones is informed of the requirement that she should leave by Mr Smith, a hospital administrator. The question for consideration here is whether he is authorised to make this pronouncement, as where powers are conferred by statute the general rule is 'delegatus non potest delegare' – a delegate cannot delegate: *Barnard v National Dock Labour Board* (9). In this instance the power under the National Health Act 1996 has been delegated to the area health authorities. The Western Area Health Authority (WAHA) is therefore a delegate: has WAHA delegated its powers to Mr Smith? It is submitted that this is not the case as there is no evidence that Mr Smith made the decision; one is only told that he notified Mrs Jones. If, however, he made the decision then it would be unlawful delegation.

The next issue to consider is one of procedural impropriety. Is Mrs Jones being deprived of her 'right' to stay in the hospital without having an opportunity to advance her case?

The statute lays down no procedures to be followed. A procedure may, however, be implied from the common law. While the court might not be willing to elevate the case of Mrs Jones to one of denial of natural justice and demand that she has a hearing, nevertheless the Health Authority is obliged to act fairly. That is, to act without bias taking into account all the relevant matters: *Re HK (An Infant)* (10). This is not the case here as Mr Smith is presumably unaware of Mrs Jones' lack of living relatives. It might be the case that Mrs Jones being an in-patient at the hospital has a legitimate expectation that she will be able to put her case before a decision is reached. A legitimate expectation may be created by deeds (as in this case when she is admitted to the hospital): *R v Secretary of State for Health, ex parte US Tobacco International Inc* (11).

Finally, Mrs Jones may be able to argue that the WAHA has failed in its discretion in deciding to close the two hospital wards reserved for elderly patients. This is a blanket decision not based upon the needs of the patients and not protecting the health of the residents in the area. If a policy is adopted which effectively prevents the relevant institution from examining the merits of individual cases this will prevent the authority from exercising its discretion and render the decision ultra vires: *British Oxygen Co v Board of Trade* (12).

Mrs Brown, on behalf of her son, will have strong grounds to challenge the decision of Wellbeing Hospital. First, is the hospital entitled to refuse the admission of Toby as it appears to be based upon a reason which goes against the statutory duty? While as has been pointed out (13), the courts are reluctant to become involved in matters of opinion over the allocation of resources, this action appears to be in clear violation of the statutory duty to maintain adequate hospital beds. Mrs Brown should quote the decision and reasoning in the *Padfield* case. Moreover, the decision has been made by the Wellbeing Hospital rather than the Area Health Authority. In this unlawful delegation (14)? A rigid adherence to the rule would indicate that it is. The courts, have, however, adopted a pragmatic approach to this and have acknowledged that when dealing with a bureaucracy delegation is inevitable, and acceptable provided that the delegate does not make policy. This has been examined in relation to the role of civil servants (*Carltona v Commissioner of Works* (15)) and would be applicable here. The hospital is not making policy but is merely implementing the policy of closing beds for pre- or post-operative intensive care. As Toby is in need of surgery he obviously falls into one or other or both categories.

Mrs Brown will have a stronger case in arguing that the decision is unreasonable as it will seriously affect Toby's chance of a full recovery. Unreasonableness is a word which occupies a considerable amount of space when discussing administrative law decisions and is based on the seminal case of *Associated Provincial Picture Houses Ltd* v *Wednesbury Corporation* (16). In the course of his judgment Lord Green MR held:

> '... if a decision on a competent matter is so unreasonable that no reasonable authority could ever have come to it then the courts can interfere ...'

He did, however, emphasise the caveat that to prove a case of that kind would require something overwhelming, a decision such that no reasonable body of persons could have come to. In this instance Mrs Brown might be able to show that as Toby's chance of recovery is going to be seriously affected then the decision is unreasonable, but the Court of Appeal in *Wednesbury* did emphasise that they should be slow to substitute their own judgment for that of the authority making the decision. In addition, as the doctor giving Mrs Brown his opinion is a family friend the court might question the impartiality of the advice. Mrs Brown will be well advised to seek a separate opinion from a medical practitioner who has no personal or family relationship.

Thus far it has been assumed that this problem is a matter of public law as it involves of public body. As the WAHA is performing a public function and there is no evidence of either Mrs Jones or Brown paying hospital fees it would fall into that category. The likely outcome for a 'successful' (ie for the applicant) judicial review will result in most cases in a quashing of the decision, and in this case the hospital authority would be told to consider the matter again upon the correct grounds. However, if the court disapproved of the action, but it raised no issue of injustice, then the remedy would not be given. Such an event is unlikely in this instance. Both parties should be aware that they have a maximum of three months to bring an action.

References

(1) [1982] AC 617
(2) (1996) The Independent 30 October
(3) (1984) The Times 14 April
(4) [1968] AC 997
(5) *R v Secretary of State for the Environment, ex parte Norwich City Council* [1982] QB 808
(5) [1925] AC 578
(6) [1982] 2 WLR 62
(7) [1976] QB 629
(8) [1978] 1 WLR 1

References (continued)

(9) [1953] 2 QB 18
(10) [1967] 2 QB 617
(11) [1992] QB 353
(12) [1971] AC 610
(13) See reference (5) and discussion above
(14) See reference (9) and discussion above
(15) [1943] 2 All ER 560. See also *R* v *Secretary of State for the Home Department, ex parte Doody* [1994] 1 AC 531
(16) [1948] 1 KB 223